FORT DAVIS

Library of Congress Cataloging-in-Publication Data

Wooster, Robert, 1956–
    Fort Davis: outpost on the Texas frontier / by Robert Wooster
      p.   cm.   —(Fred Rider Cotten popular history series; no. 8)
    Includes bibliographical references.
    ISBN 0-87611-139-8
    1. Fort Davis (Tex. : Fort)—History. I. Title. II. Series.
    F394.F63W65   1994
    976.4'145—dc20   94-2944
                                                             CIP

Published by the Texas State Historical Association in cooperation with the Center for Studies in Texas History at the University of Texas at Austin.

Cover: *Canyon, Fort Davis—I* (detail) by Capt. Arthur T. Lee, Eighth U.S. Infantry, ca. 1855. Watercolor, 4¾ x 7⅞ inches. *Courtesy Rush Rhees Library, University of Rochester.*

Fort Davis

*Outpost on the
Texas Frontier*

By Robert Wooster

Texas State
Historical Association

CONTENTS

1.
OUTPOST ON THE LIMPIA

JULIUS FROBEL, a German traveler, conducted an extensive tour of the Americas from 1850 to 1857. During the course of his wanderings, Frobel crossed the Davis Mountains of West Texas. "Nature appears here," he wrote of the region, "more than anywhere else I have seen, like a landscape-painter, composing a picture with the most simple yet refined taste." Most observers have agreed with Frobel, finding the air crisp and clean, the climate salubrious, and the surrounding elevations just high enough to be fairly called mountains yet low enough to be scaled by even the faintest of heart. With more water than the arid plains which encircle the canyons and peaks, the Fort Davis area offers a comfortable oasis amidst the vast Trans-Pecos region of Texas.[1]

Pictograph displays which confirm the presence of humans over thirteen hundred years ago are located less than forty miles northwest of Fort Davis. Five centuries later, Puebloan tribes began expanding southward from New Mexico down the Rio Grande, overwhelming the less-organized cultures of the indigenous populace. Many of the newer arrivals clustered in villages around La Junta, the junction of the Rios Concho and Grande. Known variously as Patarabueyes or Jumanos, these peoples, numbering about ten thousand, spoke a Uto-Aztecan dialect.[2]

By the mid-sixteenth century, the Mescalero Apaches had also moved into the Southwest. Fiercely independent and nomadic, small bands of Mescaleros formed loose coalitions around a male leader. As this position was neither hereditary nor permanent, an effective leader depended upon eloquence, bravery, performance, and generosity to organize a workable coalition. Sexual divisions characterized work responsibilities. Women gathered and stored wild plants and foodstuffs, made clothing, collected fuel, prepared meals, cared for children, and maintained the teepee or wickiup, a portable brush shelter. Men hunted, raided, defended the band, and, after the Spanish introduced horses, guarded the group's mounts.[3]

Warfare was vital to Apache culture. Bows and arrows, spears, axes, knives, and clubs formed the basic weapons of war until the introduction of muskets and rifles. Small parties raided isolated enemies and picked off weakly defended goods and herds, avoiding battle when the odds seemed unfavorable. The Mescaleros often allied with their eastern neighbors, the Lipan Apaches, to launch devastating strikes against the Jumanos and later the Spanish, Mexicans, and Americans.

Drawn by dreams of mineral wealth, pastoral riches, and Christianizing the native peoples, the Spanish pushed into northern Chihuahua during the sixteenth and early seventeenth centuries. But the newcomers also brought slave hunters and deadly new diseases. With local resources strained by the Spanish influx, the Jumanos grew increasingly restive. Although constrained by imperial decline, Spain's fear of French intrusion combined with continued Apache raids against mining and agricultural communities further south to necessitate action in the Trans-Pecos. Missions were established at La Junta, supported at various times by military presidios and even offensive campaigns. But the poorly equipped soldiers of the northern presidial garrisons stood little chance against the more mobile Apaches; the precipitous population decline at La Junta, attributable to wars, slave raids, migration into Mexico, and new diseases, deprived Spain of potential allies and Christian converts.[4]

In 1821, Mexico secured its independence from Spain. Frequent changes in government, however, made it difficult for the young nation to attend to its northern frontiers. A penal colony near pre-

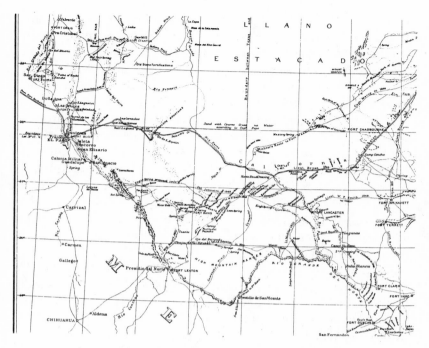

This excerpt from the army's "Map of Texas and Part of New Mexico . . ." traced the military's efforts to map and explore the Trans-Pecos during the 1850s. *Courtesy National Archives.*

sent-day Ruidosa replaced the crumbling Spanish complex at La Junta. But the garrison, consisting largely of criminals assigned to protect the frontier but themselves under a heavy guard, inspired little confidence. Few monies found their way to the frontier presidios and manpower levels rarely approached authorized strengths. Although the government awarded several land grants, immigration remained sporadic.[5]

But changes were brewing to the north. Comanche and Apache strikes into Mexico increased after the United States removed eastern Indians to present-day Oklahoma. American merchants entered into lucrative trade with the raiders, exchanging guns and ammunition for stolen booty. The aggressive policies of the

Republic of Texas, which won its independence from Mexico in 1836, created more problems. By 1846, the Chihuahuan legislature admitted: "We travel the roads . . . at their [the Indians'] whim; we cultivate the land where they wish and in the amount they wish; we use sparingly things they have left to us until the moment that it strikes their appetite to take them for themselves."[6]

Following the war against Mexico (1846–1848), Mexico formally ceded its Trans-Pecos claims to the United States. Seeking trails to gold-rich California and a route for a transcontinental railroad, Americans pushed west of the Pecos River. From San Antonio, Ranger Capt. Jack Hays's column nearly starved to death in the Big Bend before reaching Fort Leaton, where Ben Leaton, a trader along the Santa Fe-Chihuahua City trail and claimant by marriage to a huge Mexican land grant, had set up operations as de facto customs agent and rancher.

The U.S. Army was also on the move. In 1849, Lts. William H. C. Whiting and William F. "Baldy" Smith followed up the Hays trail. Between the Pecos River and Presidio del Norte, they encountered a small stream which Whiting dubbed the Limpia. Next lay Wild Rose Pass, which Whiting named in tribute to the spectacular flowers then in bloom. Just beyond the pass, the team located a grove of cottonwood trees on the edge of an open plain near the Limpia. They called the place "Painted Comanche Camp" for the pictographs that decorated some of the trees. Following an 1852 inspection tour, Col. Joseph K. F. Mansfield recommended that the military occupy the strategically located Painted Comanche Camp, which boasted water, grass, and wood, and might protect the burgeoning traffic to California and Presidio del Norte. However, the army—whose eleven thousand men were already overextended, chronically understaffed, and virtually without strategic direction—did not respond until October 1854, when a column led by Bvt. Maj. Gen. Persifor Smith reached the Limpia Creek.[7]

Formerly a prominent New Orleans attorney, Smith had raised a regiment of volunteers and fought in the Second Seminole War in Florida. During the early stages of the war with Mexico he distinguished himself in combat at Monterrey and again during the campaign against Mexico City; he now commanded the military

The parade ground and Hospital Canyon at Fort Davis during the 1850s, as captured in a watercolor by Capt. Arthur T. Lee. *Courtesy Rush Rhees Library, University of Rochester.*

Department of Texas. Smith established a military post at Painted Comanche Camp, calling it Fort Davis in honor of then-Secretary of War Jefferson Davis. Hoping to protect the garrison from winter northers, Smith tucked the fort into a canyon flanked on three sides by sheer rock walls. Commanding the post, which initially included six companies and headquarters, field staff, and band of the Eighth Infantry Regiment, was Lt. Col. Washington Seawell. A career military man and West Point graduate, Seawell feared that Indians could fire down into the site from the overlooking cliffs. Despite Seawell's objections, construction began in accord with Smith's guidelines.[8]

Like most frontier forts, Fort Davis had no wooden palisades, its structures instead forming a rough square around an open parade ground. "There is nothing to prevent Indians or anyone else, from riding through the posts in any direction," remembered one officer. "They are placed so as to have a level place for a parade, convenient to water & c., without any expectation that they will ever

In addition to his watercolors, Captain Lee drew a series of sketches of Fort Davis. The sutler's store appears in the foreground. *Courtesy Rush Rhees Library, University of Rochester.*

have to stand a siege." The troops provided most of the labor, using local building materials whenever possible. Although Congress had appropriated one hundred thousand dollars for West Texas forts, bureaucratic red tape slowed disbursement of these funds, forcing many garrison members to remain in tents. Lt. Albert J. Myer made the best of the situation by dividing his main tent into three "rooms." He explained facetiously that canvas was "the best building material in this climate." He continued wryly, "it is very tight and warm and I have often thought how cozily I am fixed." Myer took the discomfort in stride for, as he had already acknowledged, "a man gets used to taking things cooly [*sic*] after a little service with the army."[9]

As time passed, picket *jacales,* consisting of oak and cottonwood slabs set up lengthwise about a rude frame chinked with mud and prairie grass, became the norm. The enlisted men's barracks stood fifty-six feet long by twenty feet wide. Officers enjoyed separate quarters—Lt. Zenas R. Bliss's house, for example, was fifteen feet

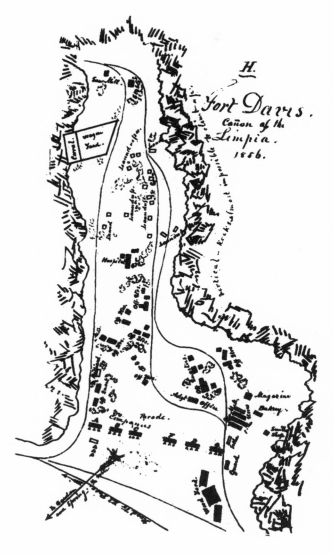

Col. J. K. F. Mansfield's outline of Fort Davis, 1856. *Courtesy Fort Davis Archives.*

square and six feet high. The structure's canvas roof and warped walls provided an unanticipated source of ventilation, welcomed until the first snows poured through the cracks.[10]

In the summer of 1856, more permanent construction was initiated during Lieutenant Colonel Seawell's temporary absence. Command had fallen to Capt. Arthur T. Lee, a multitalented individual who dabbled in art, history, music, engineering, and architecture. Lee requested from departmental superiors "permission to erect such structures as will protect the comd. during the approaching winter." The army insisted that Lee's program be of a temporary nature, but construction assumed a life of its own. By January 1857 Lee reported that six new enlisted men's barracks at the mouth of the canyon had replaced the old *jacales*. Sixty feet by twenty feet, each stone barracks had a thatched roof and flagged stone floors. The commanding officer's thirty-eight by twenty-foot frame house had two rooms and two glazed windows. Quarters for married enlisted men, kitchens, mess halls, and hospital remained in dilapidated condition, but Lee's initiative had improved material conditions for most post personnel. The outpost on the Limpia now stood as one of the army's most impressive western positions.[11]

2.
FRONTIER CHALLENGES AND CIVIL WAR

AT ITS HEIGHT during the mid-1850s, Fort Davis, boasting a garrison of over four hundred soldiers, stood among the army's largest frontier posts. But supplying, equipping, clothing, and staffing western forts, particularly one as large at Fort Davis, confounded expert and casual observer alike. Hoping to resolve these problems, Secretary of War Jefferson Davis imported more than seventy camels to Texas, where they roamed the Southwest on experimental expeditions from their base at Camp Verde, Texas. About sunrise on July 17, 1857, a party of twenty-five camels en route to Arizona reached Fort Davis. In a dramatic understatement, the commander of the exotic pilgrimage noted that "we were kindly treated by the officers." Indeed they must have been, for the sight of the camels and their Arabian handlers surely interrupted the dog days of the West Texas summer. Another diarist came closer to capturing the true spirit of the occasion when he reported that "a number of young gentlemen" returned to camp in the wee hours of the night "with a gait that denoted a slight indulgence in alcoholic stimulants."[12]

This group left the following afternoon, but Fort Davis remained a base of operations and source of manpower for subsequent camel trials. In every test, the beasts carried greater burdens while requiring less water or food than horses, mules, or oxen. Yet few handlers could tolerate the camels' bad odor, voluminous sneezing, or fierceness during rutting season. And the departure of Jefferson Davis from the War Department deprived the camels of their most powerful champion. Amidst the growing sectional crisis, interest in the camels waned; they had been sold, lost, or largely forgotten by the outbreak of the Civil War.[13]

Weapons development and distribution compounded the army's western dilemma. During the early 1850s, the infantry-dominated garrison at Fort Davis carried the Model 1842 Percussion Musket, a .69-caliber weapon weighing just over nine pounds. The design of the minié ball enabled the army to intro-duce rifled weaponry in large numbers, with the .58 caliber Model 1855 Rifle also featuring an improved paper primer system. But the new equipment took time to reach the frontiers. During his 1856 inspection, for example, Mansfield found that only thirty-three of the 442 muskets at Fort Davis had the new primer system. Only four rifles were available. While the post magazine held forty-nine thousand powder and ball cartridges, it had only 4,510 minié balls.[14]

Equally lacking were suitable uniforms, for official army issues were singularly inappropriate for West Texas. According to 1851 regulations, dark blue woolen frock coats and sky-blue trousers comprised the basic design. Trim, facings, and piping were col-ored according to the individual's service branch, with infantry wearing light blue, mounted rifles emerald green, artillery red, dragoons orange, and cavalry yellow. Though inspiring in its Napoleonic appearance, the dark blue shako, trimmed with pom-pons and bands of corresponding service colors, scarcely served the western soldier's needs, for its narrow leather visor neither shaded the eyes nor protected the neck from the Texas sun.[15]

To save money, the uniform was to be worn on all occasions. Inevitably, however, shortages in official garments plagued the Fort Davis garrison. Nearly every company on post reported insufficient stores of trousers during Colonel Mansfield's 1856 inspection. And of the 251 men assembled on parade, 149 were without their official shakos—undoubtedly having "lost" their headgear in the line of duty. The heavy woolen uniforms were regularly discarded for more comfortable garb, especially when campaigning. "White pants and summer clothes generally have usurped the woolens," acknowledged Lt. Edward L. Hartz.[16]

The War Department's lack of responsiveness to western conditions was also evident in its clumsy attempts to defeat the Indians. Theorists rarely saw the wars against Indians as important enough to merit serious intellectual study. Official manuals and West Point courses alike thus concentrated on engineering and conventional tactics rather than Indian conflicts. As such, the army developed neither strategic nor tactical plans applicable to frontier settings, a deficiency which compared unfavorably to the Indians' determination to tailor their style of warfare to the surrounding terrain.[17]

Some problems lay beyond the army's control. The inability (or refusal) of federal and state governments to establish effective, workable Indian policy meant that violence would characterize relations between Indians and non-Indians in the Fort Davis region. Public distrust of a large standing military meant that even after a substantial increase in 1855, the antebellum army numbered less than eighteen thousand men. And since cavalry units were more expensive than foot soldiers, the army's composition—four artillery, ten infantry, and five mounted regiments—rendered pursuit of tribes deemed hostile by the federal government a dubious prospect.

Confrontations had occurred even as General Smith was selecting the site for Fort Davis. En route to the Limpia, Smith had detached Capt. John G. Walker with fifty men to follow up an Indian trail. Pushing southwest from Eagle Springs toward the Rio Grande, Walker's command ran smack into the middle of an Apache encampment of sixty to seventy lodges. "The sides of the mountains were literally covered with mounted and dismounted warriors," Walker recalled, "with the women and children escaping from the village." The soldiers destroyed the lodges, along with large quantities of beef, before retreating. Walker's losses included one killed and two wounded; he estimated Indian casualties at about twenty. Smith proclaimed that Walker's "spirited action" was "to his credit and that of his command. His own conduct is spoken of in the highest terms by all present and his clothes which are cut in more than ½ by the Indian arrows bear testimony of his having been in the thickest of the fight."[18]

But distances, aridity, and the availability of escape routes to Mexico or the reservation near Fort Stanton, New Mexico, made duplicating even Walker's incomplete triumph rare. Comprised largely of Eighth Infantrymen, the antebellum Fort Davis garrison lacked the mobility and single-minded determination necessary to catch mounted Indians. Post surgeon Albert J. Myer described a typical effort. "Infantry on foot after Indians on horseback," he muttered. "They were near enough, at one time, to fire and they did so, injuring, they say, two warriors, very badly, but after a long race in a broiling sun they came back utterly exhausted."[19]

Sporadic Indian attacks on emigrants and government mail parties continued. On July 24, 1857, sixty Indians struck Sgt. Ernest Schroeder's thirteen-man mail party and wood-gathering team twenty-five miles west of Fort Lancaster, located near the junction of Live Oak Creek and the Pecos River. "Look out Sergt for the sons of bitches they will get the advantage of you if they can & dont put yourself in danger," screamed one soldier as the bluecoats scrambled for cover. The next volley indeed felled Schroeder with a shot through the heart. Surrounded and outnumbered, the soldiers began a fighting retreat, carrying Schroeder's limp frame for over a mile. As the Indians assembled for another charge, the remaining sergeant ordered his men to leave the body "& look out for ourselves." The frightened escort limped back into Fort Lancaster about three o'clock the next morning.[20]

In response, Lt. Edward L. Hartz led forty infantrymen, many of whom had been dispatched on mail escort duty from Davis, out from Fort Lancaster. Realizing that his foot soldiers could not catch the mounted Indian ambushers and that the unusually large size of his force might discourage any attacks, Hartz hid most of the command in wagons. The ruse worked. Thinking the Hartz column a regular supply train, three dozen Mescaleros struck about forty-five miles west of Lancaster. Meeting unexpectedly stiff resistance, the Apaches soon withdrew, setting the prairies afire to cover their retreat. Hartz and his men had conducted themselves well, but the inability to organize an effective pursuit

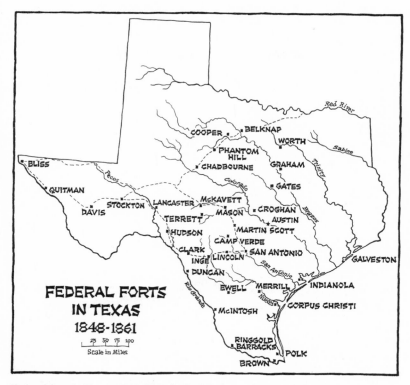

Federal forts in Texas, 1848–1861, by Jack Jackson. *Courtesy Jack Jackson.*

galled the young lieutenant. "The powerlessness of infantry to act with advantage against the bands at present infesting the road," complained Hartz, "shows conclusively that the Indians are in virtual possession of the road . . . having the power to retire beyond the reach of chastisement at their pleasure."[21]

In response to a May 1858 loss of government mules attributed to Mescalero theft near Fort Davis, Seawell ordered Lt. William B. Hazen to "overtake and chasten" the Indians. During his long military career, Hazen, a contentious man whose skeptical views

A career military man, William B. Hazen spent much of his life in the American West. Here he is captured as a colonel, during the Civil War. *National Archives photo no. 111-13-4698, courtesy Marvin E. Kroeker.*

about the environment rankled western boosters, would rise to the rank of major general of volunteers. But now the twenty-eight-year-old lieutenant faced a dangerous job. With thirty soldiers, twelve horses, and two Tejano guides, Hazen pushed on to the Guadalupe Mountains, where the party destroyed a Mescalero encampment and uncovered fifty scalps.

Yet the grueling march through the summer heat back to Davis nearly ruined Hazen's inexperienced patrol. One night, panicky guards, thinking an Indian attack imminent, shot two of their own men. Upon his return to Fort Davis, a furious Hazen commended three soldiers and the two scouts but damned the remainder of his command. "I never saw so worthless a set of men thrown together before in my life," he reported.[22]

Trying to quell the attacks against non-Indians, in 1858 the army established Fort Quitman seventy miles southeast of El Paso on the Rio Grande. The following year, the army erected Fort Stockton at the junction of the Lower El Paso Road and the Great Comanche Trail, seventy-two miles east of Fort Davis. But garrisoning the new posts proved difficult, and troops from Fort Davis were siphoned off to Quitman and Stockton. When Colonel Mansfield returned to Davis for another inspection in October 1860, he found that Seawell, still nominal post commander, had been away serving on a court-martial for the past three months. A lieutenant, three noncommissioned officers, and nineteen privates had been temporarily detached to Quitman; another officer was at San Antonio. This left Fort Davis with one officer and thirty enlisted men. Of these, ten soldiers were on extra duty and another seven privates in confinement, leaving one officer and thirteen men available for purely military tasks. This condition, common to the army's frontier posts, led one traveler to conclude that while forts were as welcome "as the oasis in the desert," "a parade of the entire force would sometimes diminish our feeling of security."[23]

Political events further complicated the federal government's efforts to control the Trans-Pecos. In late 1860 and early 1861, news of Abraham Lincoln's presidential election and the secession of South Carolina swept through the Lone Star state. In March, the commander of the Department of Texas, Georgia-born Gen. David E. Twiggs, embittered by Lincoln's election and his own repeated run-ins with commanding general Winfield Scott, surrendered all

Assistant Surgeon DeWitt C. Peters. *Courtesy Fort Davis Archives.*

federal posts in Texas to agents of the state secession convention. The twenty-six hundred troops in the state, comprising nearly 15 percent of the regular army, were to keep their small arms and be allowed safe passage to the North. From Fort Davis, Assistant Surgeon DeWitt C. Peters joined a chorus of officers critical of Twiggs's surrender. "I am one of those . . . who cannot longer regard Genl Twiggs as a veteran, or a Hero," wrote Peters, who admitted that "a few officers have resigned but that is to be expected." In the end, ten of the thirty-one officers stationed at Fort Davis before the Civil War joined the Confederate army. The enlisted personnel, however, remained overwhelmingly loyal to the Union.[24]

The Federals evacuated Fort Davis in April, with the garrison joining a four-hundred-man column which included the troops from Forts Bliss, Quitman, and, eventually, Stockton. News of the firing on Fort Sumter, South Carolina, ended the uneasy truce in Texas. On May 9, 1861, the regulars surrendered to fifteen hundred Texans twenty miles west of San Antonio. Most of the officers accepted parole the following year, but the enlisted men were not exchanged until February 1863.[25]

Having long complained about the federal government's inability to defeat the Indians, the Texans now found themselves responsible for their own protection. Small squads of state troops reoccupied many of the old federal posts; Lt. Col. John R. Baylor, a former Indian agent who had been dismissed from federal service for his animosity toward his charges, hoped to liberate southern New Mexico and Arizona for the Confederacy. As one delightfully semiliterate volunteer remaining at Davis explained, "ther are only 20 men at the post now the others are gone with . . . Col Baylor in persait of them northern troops."[26]

But Baylor's offensive left western Texas vulnerable to Indian attack. On the night of August 4, Apaches raided a cattle pen near Fort Davis. Lt. Reuben E. Mays and thirteen men trailed the Indians for over a hundred miles to the southeast until August 11, when an ambush wiped out all but one of the patrol. The defeat convinced Baylor to strengthen positions along the road to El Paso, and by late September Fort Davis housed three officers and nearly seventy enlisted men. But the volunteers soon tired of garrison life. "I think when ever I git home," speculated one dispirited Texan, "I will be able to bye me a farm and settle myself for life for I think the war will be all over by that time and if it is not I know not what I shel do."[27]

But the Confederates did not intend to assume the defensive. Having resigned his commission in the United States Army to join the Confederacy, Henry Hopkins Sibley convinced President Jefferson Davis that a Rebel invasion of New Mexico could be self-supporting and might precipitate the fall of California. Forced to retreat by the loss of its supply train at the Battle of Glorieta Pass on March 28, 1862, Sibley's Army of New Mexico quickly disintegrated. Upon receiving word of Baylor's order that subordinates "use all means to persuade the Apaches or any tribe to come in for the purpose of making peace, and when you get them together kill all the grown Indians and take the children prisoners," Confederate authorities also stripped the latter of command.[28]

In August 1862, a Federal counterthrust led the Confederates to evacuate all posts west of Fort Clark. Capt. E. D. Shirland, First California Cavalry, led a small Union patrol into Fort Davis late that month. The Federals found one arrow-ridden body at the overland mail station. Three of the military buildings had been burned or destroyed and everything of value looted. Shirland soon retraced his steps back to El Paso, skirmishing with a small party of Indians west of Dead Man's Hole on the way. But with Federals satisfied with holding El Paso and Texans preoccupied with Union invasions along their state's coastal and eastern frontiers, permanent garrisons were withdrawn from the Trans-Pecos. In the military's absence, non-Indian movement for the remainder of the Civil War grew increasingly risky.[29]

3.
REESTABLISHING THE
FEDERAL PRESENCE

ALTHOUGH THE CONFEDERACY collapsed in 1865, the need to establish the federal government's supremacy in the South delayed the return of regular troops to West Texas. In the interim, Congress slowly reorganized the nation's ground forces. By 1869, the army had been reduced to twenty-five infantry, ten cavalry, and five artillery regiments. Subsequent measures set an effective ceiling of twenty-seven thousand men. The reduced postwar army included four regiments (the Ninth and Tenth Cavalry and the Twenty-fourth and Twenty-fifth Infantry) consisting of black enlisted personnel, each of which was eventually posted at Fort Davis. Only after federal control over the former Confederate states seemed increasingly certain did the War Department begin shifting troops to the western frontiers. In 1867, the Ninth Cavalry spearheaded the reoccupation of the Trans-Pecos. Composed largely of former slaves, more than one-half of the Ninth Cavalry's enlisted personnel were Civil War veterans. The steady income, food, clothing, and education offered by the army seemed promising to many blacks faced with limited employment options.[30]

The Ninth Cavalry's Lt. Col. Wesley Merritt oversaw the reoccupation of Fort Davis. A thin, boyish-looking brevet major general, Merritt had compiled an outstanding Civil War combat record, and on June 29, 1867, he led Troops C, F, H, and I into the crumbling remains of Fort Davis. Federal soldiers also reestablished

Lt. Col. Wesley Merritt, commander of Fort Davis in 1867 and 1868–1869. *Courtesy Fort Davis Archives.*

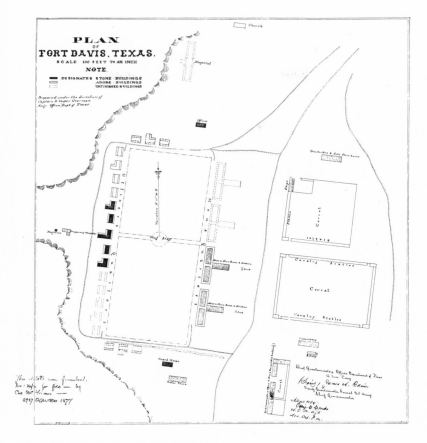

Plan of Fort Davis, 1871. *Courtesy National Archives.*

Fort Quitman as a subpost for operations into the Guadalupe Mountains. Others remained at Fort Bliss (held during the Civil War), reoccupied Forts Stockton and Clark, and staked out Fort Concho at what later became San Angelo. As Seawell had suggested a decade earlier, Lieutenant Colonel Merritt opted to rebuild Davis outside the canyon walls. But shortages in materials, mixups in army bureaucracy, and incompetent mechanics once again slowed progress, leading commanding general William T.

Sherman to admit that "the huts in which our troops are forced to live are in some places inferior to what horses usually have."[31]

Despite the obstacles at Fort Davis, by January 1871 four limestone and five adobe officers' houses formed a north-south line across the canyon mouth at Fort Davis. Each had front and back porches and a separate rear kitchen. Eleven other quarters were either under construction or projected for future development. Auxiliary buildings, including a bakery, magazine, executive office building, quartermaster and commissary storehouses, guardhouse, and hospital, were in various states of construction, repair, or planning. Six companies of unmarried enlisted men crowded into two barracks, each 186 by 27 feet. A twelve-foot passageway separated each barrack into two equal sections and led to a rear extension, which included a mess room, kitchen, and storeroom. One cavalry troop still lived in tents; married men and laundresses were also without permanent quarters.[32]

Regulations concerning official military uniforms became slightly more responsive to West Texas conditions following the Civil War. With the gradual depletion of surplus wartime stocks, new uniforms were adopted in 1872. Looser fitting dark-blue coats and broad-brimmed hats keyed the new issues, although financial exigencies, field experience, and climatic demands meant that few units sported full regulation outfits. In belated response to the criticism heaped upon wool uniforms, cork helmets, experimental cotton duck uniforms, muslin shirts, and white cotton trousers were tested during the 1880s.[33]

Model 1873 Springfield rifles and carbines were standard issue shoulder arms in the post-Civil War years. Though some complained about their single-shot capacity, most observers believed these reliable .45-caliber breech-loaders served the army well until 1892, when the War Department adopted its first standard magazine rifles. Cavalrymen carried a .45-caliber Colt 1872 six-shooter. Light, easily managed, and accurate at ranges up to four thousand yards, the 1.65-inch Hotchkiss "mountain gun" howitzer added long-range punch. Less successful was the hopper-fed Gatling gun, which could fire 350 rounds per minute by virtue of its ten revolving barrels. But the weapon's short range, proclivity to jam, and cumbersome carriage limited its use.[34]

Attempting to insure that soldiers enjoyed at least a few amenities, the War Department authorized post sutlers to set up stores on army posts. In exchange, these merchants paid a tax to post authorities and set prices according to rates established by a board of officers. Alexander Young had held the position at Davis before the Civil War; although one irate civilian asserted that Young hawked his wares "at enormous prices," sharp-eyed inspector Mansfield reported that the sutler kept his store "well supplied with all the requisites for the troops & gives satisfaction."[35]

During the 1870s, the system fell victim to the corrupt administration of Secretary of War William Belknap, who brazenly lined his own pockets by selling the traderships. Belknap was forced to resign in 1876, but not before garrison members had universally condemned his appointees at Fort Davis. Backed by an Ohio congressman, John D. Davis and George H. Abbott secured the new appointment. By the early 1880s their compound consisted of a residence, shed, bar, store, telegraph office, and two privies. Although the traders were on occasion reprimanded—usually for selling "poor" whiskey or allowing undesirable elements to use their bar and billiard table—Davis and Abbott seem to have satisfied the garrison's needs until 1887, when a nonprofit, government-sponsored canteen was opened.[36]

With the War Department having made few provisions for retired military personnel, several former soldiers settled in the nearby civilian community which grew up around the federal post. Archie Smith, a Tenth Cavalry veteran, married a native of Mexico and became a prosperous cattleman. Another former soldier, Charles Mulhern, returned with his wife to Fort Davis upon his 1885 discharge, where he managed other soldiers' real estate interests in addition to running his own ranch.[37]

Although entrepreneurs from Fort Stockton and San Antonio dominated army contracts let at Davis, a bustling community of nearly one thousand persons developed in and around the Limpia and Toyah valleys. Businesses clustered around the courthouse south of the fort proper. In 1884, the town boasted a drug store, lumber yard, clock shop, dressmaker, bakery, butcher's shop, stable, liquor store, two saloons, two groceries, two hotels, and seven dry goods stores. A local Masonic lodge chapter had recently been organized, and the inaugural issue of a local newspaper, *The Apache Rocket*, had appeared in May 1882. Representatives from several denominations ministered to the community's religious needs.[38]

Class and racial divisions stratified the town. Whites dominated the skilled and professional classes, but two-thirds of the civilians had Hispanic surnames. Many Mexican Americans lived east of the central business district in a district known as Chihuahua. Described by one white observer as a "squalid little Mexican settlement," Chihuahua's saloons, gambling houses, and brothels attracted soldiers thirsting for action of a nonmilitary nature. Officers avoided this area, preferring the company of Anglo ranchers like Daniel Murphy and George and Lizzie Crosson.[39]

The development of local government bolstered the nonmilitary community. In 1875, the state legislature organized Presidio County, with Fort Davis as county seat. Ten years later, voters transferred the county seat to the burgeoning railroad town of Marfa, situated some twenty miles to the south. As a consolation prize, Fort Davis retained the county jail. A protest before the state supreme court failed, but a separate Jeff Davis County, with its own county seat at Fort Davis, was created in 1887. Tensions still ran high during the following year's presidential contest, with local campaigners allegedly bribing voters with free soda water.[40]

Fort Davis once again became a thriving frontier post. As had been the case before the Civil War, building projects continued to play a major role in garrison life. In addition to the members of the army units stationed at Fort Davis, considerable numbers of laundresses, wives, and children roamed the post grounds. But the reestablishment of the federal presence also encouraged the growth of another community, associated with but separate from the post proper. Thus the army's decision to reoccupy its outpost on the Limpia, as was so often true for western military establishments, also sparked a permanent civilian presence.

4.
LIFE AT A
FRONTIER OUTPOST

ON THE MILITARY POST ITSELF, reveille rousted enlisted personnel just after daybreak, with short drills initiated shortly thereafter. Breakfast, generally consisting of coffee, bacon, bread, and molasses, was served in the mess halls at about seven o'clock. An hour later, officers organized the daily guard. Inspection of company barracks began about nine o'clock; the officer of the day handled routine sanitation, sentinel, and guardhouse activities. For the enlisted men, selection to the guard meant closer supervision yet merited minor privileges like the chance to skip drills. Fatigue details, on the other hand, were seen as more burdensome. Although such extra duty meant additional income, most soldiers resented the unmilitary nature of these activities.

Lunch call, featuring hearty servings of beef or pork, bread, and coffee, heralded the day's major meal. Standard vegetables included rice, peas, or beans. Fresh produce from the post garden or supplies purchased from post and company funds occasionally filled the void, but deficiencies in the official ration, lax inspection, inadequate storage facilities, and poor cooks took a heavy toll. Over a six-month period in 1874–1875, for example, a Fort Davis board of officers condemned, among other things, 900 pounds of hominy, 97 gallons of molasses, 208 pounds of vermicelli, 256 pounds of macaroni, 588 cans of condensed milk, 9 heads of cheese, 154 cans of sardines, 20 gallons of onions, 198 cans of

Fort Davis about 1886. The sutler's complex appears in the foreground. *Courtesy Fort Davis Archives.*

sweet potatoes, 120 pounds of creamed tartar, 143 cans of onions, and 848 cans of lima beans. Ill-trained cooks, drafted from the ranks and ordered to the kitchen, hampered efforts to improve the diet. As one inspector complained, "the baker . . . has never served a regular trade at the business, & this may account in some measure for the indifferent bread." Although the army made available an official cooking manual in 1883, Congress refused to provide for permanent cooks until 1898.[41]

Fatigue call reassembled work parties about one o'clock. Company drill began two hours later. Officers, many of whom had little training in such exercises, depended heavily upon their sergeants throughout these military exercises. Lt. John Bigelow, fresh from a five-year stint as temporary instructor at West Point, seemed satisfied that he could maneuver his company "with some assurance that it will not go to pieces." Bayonet practice, marching, and tactical movements predominated, with regular target

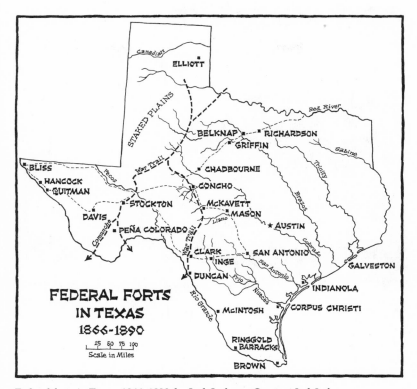

Federal forts in Texas, 1866–1890, by Jack Jackson. *Courtesy Jack Jackson.*

practice introduced only after George Custer's 1876 defeat at the Little Bighorn. Retreat sounded at sunset, followed by a light supper of warmed-over beef, bread, and coffee. Tattoo ended the day about 8:30, with Sunday morning dress parades giving the fort an especially military appearance.[42]

Medical care was problematic, with even the best doctors powerless to combat diseases whose causes they little understood. The post's system of wooden privies and dry-earth closets was ill-designed to encourage effective sanitation. Fort Davis, however,

The acerbic surgeon John V. Lauderdale with his family on the porch of their quarters at Fort Davis. *Courtesy Fort Davis Archives.*

largely escaped the ravages of scurvy, a common ailment on the Texas military frontier. The pre-Civil War hospital had drawn universal condemnation, but during the mid-1870s a twelve-bed infirmary was constructed behind officers' row.[43]

In 1869 the War Department, seeking to improve health, directed post surgeons to inspect sanitation facilities. With medical affairs seemingly in competition with military duty, surgeons and post commanders frequently disputed the attention accorded health and hygiene. During the late 1880s, for example, Assistant Surgeon John V. Lauderdale muttered that Fort Davis post commander Col. Melville A. Cochran "does not seem to know as much about looking after the interests of a Post as Barnum's fat boy." Quartermaster Joseph M. Partello, whom Lauderdale believed had diverted funds from the fort's new ice-making machine to other endeavors, was, in the doctor's words, "a selfish pig."[44]

Pay raises during the mid-1850s had set a private's minimum pay at eleven dollars a month; in 1871 Congress raised the base rate to thirteen dollars. With bonuses for longevity and reenlistment, extra duty pay, and free housing and rations, army compensation was competitive with that received by unskilled civilian laborers. Although regulations specified that military personnel be paid every two months, traveling paymasters often found meeting this schedule impossible. The paymaster's much-anticipated arrival thus sparked great excitement from troops expecting several months' back pay and allowances. Something approaching pandemonium broke out when the men received their pay, as many immediately determined to break their enforced abstinence from the delights offered by assorted gamblers, prostitutes, and merchants lured by the possibility of quick profit.[45]

Two to four laundresses, who received government rations, quarters, and fuel, handled washing chores for each company of forty to seventy men. These women collected their debts from the soldiers as the latter collected their pay. But the long intervals between the paymaster's visits sometimes left the laundresses, like their customers, badly strapped for cash. "We are a lone [sic] standing women and thought best to try for your assistance," explained two laundresses in seeking help from the post commander. Claiming that the women either themselves engaged in prostitution or harbored ladies of the evening, critics of the system forced the army to strip the laundresses of their government rations in 1883, but the women continued to function in a semiofficial capacity for many years.[46]

Regulations prohibited married men from enlisting, and those who later wished to marry needed permission from their commanding officers. Noncommissioned personnel frequently married company laundresses, but the army took a skeptical view of many alliances. Pvt. Daniel C. Robinson, whose Tenth Cavalry company served at Davis during the 1870s and 1880s, claimed his bride worked as servant for an officer. To the army, however, the "marriage" was strictly one of convenience which allowed

Robinson to live away from the enlisted barracks. "It appears that they play fast for a while," concluded one investigator, "then they play loose for a time."[47]

Officers' wives comprised a distinct class. At Fort Davis ten of the twenty-eight officers listed in the 1870 and 1880 censuses had wives living with them. Ten children were also in residence. These elite dependents rarely interacted with the laundresses or enlisted men. Complaints about the isolation and boredom of the western garrisons were common, but many women relished the frontier military experience and sought to fulfill their own ambitions by promoting their husbands' careers. The romance of the west, the challenges of army life, and the beauty of Fort Davis offered much; if they wanted to live with their officer-husbands, they had no choice but to move west. "I had 'gone for a soldier,'" wrote one officer's wife, "and a soldier I determined to be."[48]

Women bore the brunt of childrearing, as typified by the experiences of Mary Swan Thompson, wife of Lt. James K. Thompson. With their newborn infant nursing at regular hours, Mary informed her mother that "all my nervousness has gone. . . . I've not an ache or pain anywhere." But four weeks later, an exhausted Mary confided: "This is the first afternoon I've had a moment to myself in I can't tell when. . . . The baby is so wakeful all day long and keeps me so busy—but today he has just succeeded after trying for nearly two hours in howling himself to sleep . . . and there is nobody to take him but myself. So please stop scolding me about not writing."[49]

The army took limited steps to provide for the entertainment and enlightenment of the men. The Fort Davis library, for example, boasted several periodical subscriptions and over one thousand books. Regimental bands often offered popular and morale-boosting concerts. A post school flourished under the efforts of George M. Mullins, a Disciples of Christ minister and Twenty-fifth Infantry chaplain. Summing up his efforts in 1878, Mullins reported that more than 160 men had learned to read and write and had developed "a sense of self-respect and a pride of soldiership." A new post chapel, completed in 1879 and positioned on the northeast side of the parade ground, seated 250 persons.[50]

Sgt. Thomas Hall Forsyth was named commissary sergeant at Fort Davis in 1885. Here the proud father appears seated left with his wife. *Courtesy Fort Davis Archives.*

Sporadic theatrical performances added color, if not always refinement, to garrison life. "A soldiers show is usually one of protracted waits for something," explained the acerbic Lauderdale. After the Civil War, soldiers also joined fraternal organizations, including the Good Templars, the Oddfellows, and the Grand Army of the Republic. Baseball became a popular activity, with a special vigor marking contests between the Davis nine and civilian or rival garrison teams.[51]

Holidays and the arrival of visitors demanded special festivities. On Christmas Day, every company prepared a feast replete with wild game, chickens, pigs, pies, puddings, and special sauces. Card-playing, balls, hops, and socials honored the arrival of outside dignitaries. "We have enough to entertain us and prevent this happy coterie from affliction with that languer [sic] so common to the society of a frontier military post," wrote one satisfied Fort Davis correspondent.[52]

Though unified against outsiders and temporarily able to put aside their differences during special occasions and celebrations, "the idea of the army being 'one happy family,'" remembered one officer's wife, "was a considerable exaggeration." Slow promotion, interregimental and interservice rivalries, and jealousies between West Pointers and non-West Pointers (31 percent of the 259 officers known to have served at Davis after the Civil War were U.S. Military Academy graduates) divided post society. This tension was especially evident among the officers. "Some of the doings of these men are worse than anything I had imagined and too vulgar to be recorded in my journal," wrote Lt. John Bigelow Jr. Capt. Samuel Woodward called his superior, Maj. Anson Mills, "a sorry excuse"; in return, the major described his antagonist as "slow to obey."[53]

Low pay exacerbated the tensions among officers. Their basic pay—forty-five dollars per month for a second lieutenant following a raise in 1857; fourteen hundred dollars per year for a second lieutenant after the Civil War—did not begin to match what comparable occupations might have demanded in civil life, although supplemental allowances for rations, servants, horses, and special appointments somewhat bridged this gap. To save money, officers often supplied their own rations and ate in their own quarters, frequently combining their resources to form mess pools, sharing responsibilities and expenses.

Though the officers were often divided amongst themselves, social stratification and army tradition clearly distinguished them from enlisted men. As Lt. Edward L. Hartz explained, "we have no society apart from the officers." Commissioned personnel often employed slaves, servants, and soldiers from the ranks ("strikers") to assist them in household duties. Enlisted personnel rarely corresponded with the stereotypes held by many officers, who believed white, native-born lads from family farms to be the best material. Instead, the overwhelming majority of enlisted men, at Fort Davis and in the army as a whole, were either foreign-born mechanics, common laborers, or former slaves. In 1860, for example, over 40 percent of the Fort Davis garrison had been born in Ireland. After the war, the high number of blacks at Fort Davis reduced the percentage of foreign-born and increased the number of southerners. Although blacks repeatedly demonstrated their courage in battle, white officers found their presence difficult to accept, magnifying all transgressions and assailing what they perceived as the poor character of their men.[54]

Racial tensions clearly affected desertion rates at Fort Davis. In the army as a whole, desertion claimed some 15 percent of all enlisted men every year. After the Civil War, however, the problem was not always so great at Fort Davis, with its largely black garrison deserting at a rate of less than 2 percent per year from 1867 to 1880. By 1882, as the ratio of white units began to increase, desertion skyrocketed, claiming nearly 20 percent of the garrison. Not only did whites desert at higher rates, but the racial tensions between white and black soldiers apparently convinced many blacks to leave their units as well.[55]

An incident involving West Point's first black graduate, Lt. Henry Flipper, symbolized the difficulties faced by black soldiers. Born in Thomasville, Georgia, Flipper had in 1876 graduated fiftieth in his class of seventy-six. He accepted a commission in the Tenth Cavalry and served at Fort Sill, Indian Territory, until the regiment's transfer to Fort Davis in 1880. Here he served as post commissary officer. Ostracized by his fellow officers, Flipper was arrested in August 1881 for misappropriating army funds and concealing a discrepancy of some twenty-four hundred dollars in his commissary accounts. A court-martial convened the following month at the post chapel, where Flipper explained that he had planned to use the royalties from his recently published autobiography to make up the shortfall. Unfortunately, the check had been delayed, and his bank balance had been insufficient to make up the difference.

Unable to prove Flipper guilty of embezzlement, the court-martial dismissed him from the service for "conduct unbecoming an officer and a gentleman." The young man went on to become a successful mining engineer, but spent much of his remaining life futilely attempting to clear his name. A sloppy accountant, Flipper had deserved a sharp reprimand, but the severity of his punishment suggests that racism dictated the final decision. White officers guilty of comparable transgressions (which were common considering the tangle of paperwork entailed in the commissary officer's position) rarely received such a stiff penalty. Despite the excellent record compiled by black troops, the myth of black inferiority would not be shattered at Fort Davis.[56]

Lt. Henry Flipper. After his court-martial, Flipper became a successful mining engineer. *Courtesy Fort Davis Archives.*

5.
THE DEFEAT
OF THE INDIANS

ALTHOUGH ROUTINE DUTY, economic concerns, and post society dominated the everyday life of the garrison, Fort Davis's primary function remained the campaigns against the Indians. Between 1872 and 1874, a congressional committee calculated that Indians killed or captured more than two hundred whites and stole one hundred thousand cattle and horses in Texas alone. Few officers, however, understood the nature of warfare against Indians or exhibited the determination necessary to overtake the enemy. The garrison now routinely included a cavalry component, but most expeditions from Fort Davis met the fate described in an 1870 scout: "marched a distance of about 187 miles, without seeing any signs of Indians and without injury to men or stock."[57]

An unusually successful operation came in September 1868, when Lt. Patrick Cusack and two troops of Ninth Cavalrymen caught two hundred Apaches eighty miles south of the post. Suffering two wounded, Cusack claimed that his men killed or wounded between forty and sixty Indians, captured a pony herd, recovered two hundred head of stolen cattle, and freed two prisoners. On their triumphant return to Davis pranksters donned their captured booty and pretended to be Indians, surprising a group of soldiers quarrying rock just off base. "You can imagine how fast those men ran trying to get back to the post," laughed one veteran.[58]

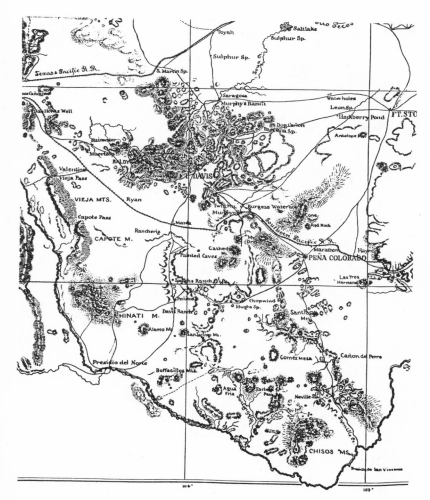

Segment of "Military Map of Texas, 1884." *Courtesy National Archives.*

Col. William ("Pecos Bill") Shafter, a huge, blustering, hard-driving man who first took command at Fort Davis in 1871, attempted to energize the garrison, insisting that active campaigning was more important than additional construction. Shafter inspired a

Col. George Andrews, longtime post commander. *Courtesy Fort Davis Archives.*

brief flurry of activity until called away to campaign along the upper Brazos River the following year. Col. George L. Andrews assumed command at Fort Davis, where he would serve, with sporadic interruptions, for six years. During Andrews's tenure, escorts for the mail parties, guards for the stage stations and local ranchers, and detachments for exploration or road- and tele-graph-building projects were more common than offensive opera-tions.[59]

Responsibilities along the Mexican border also drained the Fort Davis garrison. Filibustering groups organizing in the United States needed to be broken up, Indian attacks on both sides of the border had to be stopped, and the lives and property of U.S. citi-zens along the Rio Grande protected. To meet these challenges, detachments from Fort Davis frequently occupied Presidio. The most explosive episode came in December 1876, when complaints from U.S. businessmen convinced Colonel Andrews to dispatch a company of the Twenty-fifth Infantry and an artillery piece south to Presidio. After an American hostage was taken south of the bor-der, Andrews unlimbered the cannon and lobbed several shells onto the Mexican side of the river. The demonstration having the desired effect, the hostage was freed.[60]

Troops from Fort Davis also established subposts at Eagle Spring, Seven Springs, and in the Guadalupe Mountains. But field operations seemed uncoordinated and ranchers claimed substan-tial losses from Indian attacks. Mounting evidence suggested these raids came from New Mexico, where Victorio, Nana, and various groups of Mimbres, Chiricahua, and Mescalero Apaches opposed the government's attempts to force them to accept reservation life. The army suspected that Victorio used the Mescalero Reservation as a supply depot, recruiting ground, and safe haven. After attempts to disarm and dismount the reservation's occupants had gone awry, in 1880 Col. Benjamin Grierson, a former music teacher who had during the Vicksburg campaign led one of the Civil War's great cavalry raids, developed a new plan of action for his Tenth Cavalry. Rather than chase Victorio across the Trans-Pecos, Grierson positioned troops at strategic waterholes. Sharp skirmishes—with Grierson and a small detachment at Tinaja de las Palmas on July 30 and a larger force at Rattlesnake Springs on August 5; with other detachments led by Cpl. Asa Weaver west of Eagle Spring on August 3; and with parties under Capt. William B. Kennedy and Capt. Thomas C. Lebo on August 3 and 4—convinced Victorio to move back south of the border. Mexican troops later cornered and killed him in the Candelaria Mountains.[61]

Although Grierson's troops had failed to capture Victorio, they had harassed the famous chief out of Texas. In addition, the colonel calculated that his command had strung up 300 miles of telegraph lines, built over 1,000 miles of wagon roads, and marched 135,710 miles from 1878 to 1881. According to Grierson "a settled feeling of security" now existed in West Texas; "a rapid and permanent increase of the population and wealth" was sure to follow. Reports of Indian attacks indeed declined, with the final major encounter between Indians and non-Indians in the Fort Davis region coming in January 1882, when Texas Rangers ambushed an Apache camp near the Sierra Diablo Mountains.[62]

As Indian conflicts diminished and Forts McKavett and Stockton were abandoned, in November 1882 Grierson moved his headquarters from Fort Concho to Fort Davis. Shunned by some fellow officers for his service in a black regiment and accused by superiors of being too willing to accept Indian professions of peaceful intent, Grierson's lack of formal military training left him further isolated. Personal calamities had also taken their toll. He and his wife, Alice, had lost two children in infancy, and their thirteen-year-old daughter Edith had died of typhoid fever. Two sons, Charles and Robert, suffered mental breakdowns while attending college. In the face of this adversity, Grierson determined to protect his remaining fortunes at any cost. The bearded, sharp-eyed colonel had first seen Fort Davis during an 1878 inspection tour. "This appears to be a first rate country to go to sleep in," he had advised his wife. His Herculean efforts to develop Fort Davis neatly coincided with equally tireless attempts to provide financial and psychological security for his family. Expanding the military presence, even in the absence of a direct Indian threat, reasoned Grierson, might also increase the value of his personal investments.[63]

Benjamin Henry Grierson and Alice Kirk Grierson. *Courtesy Fort Davis Archives.*

Grierson's administration marked the height of Fort Davis's glory as a military post. At his previous commands, the colonel had overseen major expansion and construction projects; in February 1884, under his direction, Fort Davis secured its largest military complement, a paper strength of thirty-nine officers and 643 enlisted men. The bulging garrison required additional space and made more common the dread process of "ranking out," whereby senior officers forced junior officers to vacate their quarters upon demand. Alice Grierson described the process: "Capt. [Thomas C.] Lebo came in Sunday—he chose Capt. [John T.] Morrison's quarters—Morrison [newly promoted Captain Charles L.] Cooper's, and Cooper the Viele house." Apparently the "Viele house" was then occupied by the ill-fated Lt. Leighton Finley, who, being away from the post on patrol, would not find out about his eviction until he returned.[64]

Such overcrowding was made to order for Grierson, who asked for fifty-one thousand dollars to fund additional construction. Although actual appropriations did not meet Grierson's requests, the colonel plunged ahead. He initiated new commissary and quartermaster storehouses, another set of officers' quarters, two new enlisted barracks, and further hospital expansion. Conveniently enough, Grierson approved several of the projects while serving as acting commander of the Department of Texas.

With the Indian threat removed, Colonel Grierson hoped the increased army stake would spur new settlement and economic development. To capitalize on the projected increase in land prices, he eventually claimed over forty-five thousand acres in Jeff Davis, Brewster, and Presidio Counties. The real estate investments also allowed the colonel to place his sons, Robert and Charley, whose academic endeavors had seemed too stressful, in what he presumed might be a more sedate enterprise: ranching. Direct access to a railroad, the colonel reasoned, would guarantee the success of his endeavors. To connect Fort Davis with the recently built Southern Pacific line at Marfa, twenty miles south, Grierson and his sons took leading roles in the Fort Davis and Marfa Narrow Gauge Railway Company.[65]

Attracting capital for the railroad venture depended to a great extent upon the government's purchase of the Fort Davis military reservation. Washington had long relied on long-term leases for army posts in the Lone Star state; outright purchase might assure the permanent military presence demanded by investors. Grierson thus resumed negotiations with property owner John H. James. Deeming James's proposal to sell the 640 acres on which the buildings lay for nearly thirty thousand dollars "exorbitant," Grierson began "quiet financiering" with property owners north and east of the post. These men included fellow Tenth Cavalrymen George A. Brenner, the regiment's chief musician and a longtime personal friend, and Lt. Mason M. Maxon, husband of one of Grierson's nieces. But the changing nature of the colonel's proposals concerned army officials, who also recognized the reduced Indian presence. The government bought some land, but the scheme to purchase the entire site ran aground. His complex negotiations with potential railroad investors collapsed accordingly.[66]

Grierson's Tenth Cavalry, which had been stationed in West Texas since 1873, was transferred to Arizona in 1885. The colonel

Officers' row at Fort Davis, ca. 1885. *Courtesy Fort Davis Archives.*

had lobbied hard to keep his unit at Fort Davis, but superiors complained that the unit had "become 'localized' to an extent as to have an effect prejudicial to the public interest." On the afternoon of April 1, 1885, nearly the entire Tenth Cavalry assembled to leave Fort Davis in a final grand review, an impressive sight never matched in community annals. Only after his retirement in 1890 could Grierson return to Fort Davis on a semipermanent basis, dividing his time between his Fort Davis-area ranch and the family homestead in Jacksonville, Illinois, until his death in 1911.[67]

6.
TAPS

FORT DAVIS HAD LONG BEEN considered one of the army's healthiest western posts, and its moderate climate and sheltering canyon walls made it a favorite among military personnel who enjoyed the serene isolation of the Trans-Pecos. It was therefore shocking when, during the mid-1880s, medical studies revealed abnormally high rates of typhoid, dysentery, malarial fevers, and diarrhea among the post's garrison. "This is . . . somewhat of a disappointment," noted Brig. Gen. David S. Stanley, commander of the military Department of Texas, "as Fort Davis . . . has long been reckoned as a good sanitarium for Texas."[68]

An impure water supply seemed to be the problem. Grierson, the inveterate builder, had initiated an elaborate system for piping in water from the Limpia Creek. But in 1888, post surgeon John V. Lauderdale classified the water as a "thin pea soup emulsion." Additional tinkering with the filter temporarily improved water quality, but the thousands of tadpoles which thrived in the reservoir seemed impossible to remove. Runoff water from the surrounding hills, laid bare by overgrazing, also poured through the military reservation, exacerbating the situation.[69]

Changing western conditions—most notably the elimination of the Indian presence and the expansion of the railroads—further threatened the continued military occupation of Fort Davis. The twenty-odd miles to Marfa seemed just enough to make the post on the Limpia seem misplaced. In August 1887, General Stanley thus recommended the fort's abandonment. "Fort Davis is very much out of place," he advised; "it is inconvenient to get to it and to draw troops from it, and it is expensive."[70]

Hoping the consolidation of scattered western garrisons would save money, in spring 1891 Secretary of War Redfield Proctor visited several Rio Grande posts and met with Stanley at San Antonio. Upon his return to Washington, Proctor reported his findings to Rep. S. W. T. Lanham, whose Trans-Pecos district would be most affected by possible changes. Proctor believed a large El Paso post advisable; the new buildings at Fort Hancock, established in 1882 some forty miles south of El Paso, also dictated a continued army presence. On Fort Davis, however, the secretary delivered bad news: "The troops will probably be withdrawn from there before the first of July."[71]

Local residents had long feared such a move. Venerable Daniel Murphy, a longtime rancher, trader, and favorite among post officers, issued a final plea to Secretary of State James G. Blaine. To Murphy it seemed foolish to leave "the richest mineral belt on the Continent south of us to the Pacific" open "to the most unlaw abiding people of bought [both] countryes and we are liable at any time to be plased in a disagreeable pocession [position]." Fort Davis, however, enjoyed little clout with the Democrats who dominated Texas's congressional delegation; Lanham and Sen. John Reagan expressed more interest in saving other posts. Closing Fort Davis thus seemed economically sensible and politically feasible.[72]

Through the late spring and early summer of 1891, troops at Fort Davis received their transfers. Four companies of the Twenty-third Infantry were moved to Forts McIntosh and Bliss. A troop of Third Cavalrymen was dispatched along with the post library to Fort Hancock. Quartermaster stores, commissary goods, and chapel furniture were shipped to San Antonio. On June 19, everything that could not be moved was sold at public auction, which netted the government nearly three thousand dollars. Company F, Fifth Infantry, elements of which had remained to oversee the move, had departed by July 3 for Fort Sam Houston.[73]

Charles Mulhern, retired veteran now acting as estate manager for Lt. Mason M. Maxon, cogently reported the effects of the military's departure. "Plenty of houses in Davis now and no one to live in them," he wrote. "The Bottom is out." An economic depression indeed followed. Although most civilians remained, the army's once-captive market was now gone. The John James family, owner of the military reservation, was able to rent out many buildings on the former post as residences for several years, but looting and weather took their inevitable toll and the structures fell into disrepair.[74]

In 1906, the "abandoned and useless military reservation" of Fort Davis was turned over to the Department of the Interior. Although the small government tracts near the post proper were later sold, in 1959 the Advisory Board on Parks, Historic Sites, Buildings, and Monuments recommended that Fort Davis be made a part of the national park system. Two years later, that goal was realized, allowing significant restoration and preservation projects to begin.[75]

The United States army had occupied Fort Davis for nearly forty years as the nation achieved what many believed to be its manifest destiny: the conquest of a continent. In establishing and garrisoning posts like Fort Davis, the army had been a major factor in this process. In many ways, the outpost on the Limpia had typified the frontier military experience. The regulars spent more time building and performing day-to-day chores than they did fighting Indians, but the garrison's presence offered reassurance to overland emigrants and encouraged non-Indian settlement. As danger from Indian attack on the post proper was minimal, walls did not enclose the fort's sprawling buildings.

With its diverse garrisons including each of the post-Civil War army's four black regiments, Fort Davis also offers valuable insights into nineteenth-century American society. The experiences of these soldiers and their dependents, combined with the large Mexican American civilian community, reflected the stratified racial relations which accompanied the nation's westward expansion. Although frontier necessity sometimes blurred color lines, racial prejudice nonetheless permeated post society. Their ranks included many a ne'er-do-well, but the soldiers were by and large solid citizens who left a permanent imprint upon the American psyche. Limited in number and often befuddled by the Indians' hit-and-run tactics, the army rarely adopted foolproof measures, but in the end, the frontier regulars did the job assigned them by the federal government.

NOTES

Research for this project was compiled while working on a larger study of Fort Davis, Texas, through a grant from the National Park Service. Those seeking more complete references should consult Robert Wooster, *History of Fort Davis, Texas,* Southwest Cultural Resources Center, Professional Paper No. 34 (Santa Fe, 1990). The author would like to thank Richard B. McCaslin, now assistant professor of history at High Point College, North Carolina, and Mary Williams and the entire staff of the Fort Davis National Historic Site for their assistance.

1. Julius Frobel, *Seven Years' Travel in Central America, Northern Mexico, and the Far West of the United States* (London: Richard Bentley, 1859), 460.

2. W. W. Newcomb Jr., *The Indians of Texas: From Prehistoric to Modern Times* (Austin: University of Texas Press, 1961), 225–237; Michael L. Tate, *The Indians of Texas: An Annotated Research Bibliography,* Native American Bibliographic Series, No. 9 (Metuchen, N. J.: Scarecrow Press, 1986), 64–68.

3. Morris E. Opler, "The Apachean Culture Pattern and its Origins," in *Handbook of North American Indians,* ed. Alfonso Ortiz (20 vols.; Washington: Smithsonian Institution, 1983), X, 419–437.

4. Howard G. Applegate and C. Wayne Hanselka, *La Junta de los Rios del Norte y Conchos* (El Paso: Texas Western Press, 1974); John F. Bannon, *The Spanish Borderlands Frontier, 1513–1821* (New York: Holt, Rinehart, and Winston, 1970); Oakah L. Jones Jr., *Nueva Vizcaya: Heartland of the Spanish Frontier* (Albuquerque: University of New Mexico Press, 1988).

5. Carlos E. Castañeda, *Our Catholic Heritage in Texas, 1519–1936* (7 vols.; Austin: Von-Boeckmann Jones, 1936–1958), V, 114–115; Cecilia Thompson, *History of Marfa and Presidio County, Texas, 1535–1946* (2 vols.; Austin: Nortex Press, 1985), I, 36–37, 65; David J. Weber, *The Mexican Frontier, 1821–1846: The American Southwest Under Mexico,* Histories of the American Frontier (Albuquerque: University of New Mexico Press, 1982), 108–117.

6. Weber, *Mexican Frontier,* 87.

7. "Journal of Henry Chase Whiting, 1849," in Ralph P. Bieber and Averam B. Bender (eds.), *Exploring Southwestern Trails, 1846–1854*, Southwestern Historical Series, No. 7 (Glendale: Arthur H. Clark Co., 1938), 77, 331; Report of Smith, May 25, 1849, S. Exec. Doc. 64, 31st Cong., 1st sess. (Serial 562), pp. 4–7; J. K. F. Mansfield, *Mansfield on the Condition of Western Forts*, ed. Robert Frazer (Norman: University of Oklahoma Press, 1963), 28–29.

8. Jerome A. Greene, *Historic Resource Study: Fort Davis National Historic Site* (National Park Service, 1986), 11; Smith to Cooper, Oct. 9, 1854 (microfilm: Fort Davis Archives [cited hereafter as FODA]); Robert M. Utley, *Fort Davis National Historic Site, Texas*, National Park Service Historical Handbook Series no. 38 (Washington, D.C.: Department of the Interior, 1965), 6–7; Martin L. Crimmins (ed.), "Colonel J. K. F. Mansfield's Report of the Inspection of the Department of Texas in 1856," *Southwestern Historical Quarterly*, XLII (Apr., 1939), 356 (cited hereafter as *SHQ*).

9. Zenas R. Bliss Reminiscences, I, 119–120 (Center for American History, University of Texas, Austin); David A. Clary (ed.), "'I Am Already Quite a Texan': Albert J. Myer's Letters From Texas, 1854–1856," *SHQ*, LXXXII (July, 1978), 57–58.

10. Bliss Reminiscences, I, 119–120, 173–174; Edward to Father, Jan. 4, 1856, Edward L. Hartz Papers (Library of Congress, Washington, D.C.).

11. Lee to Department of Texas, Aug. 30, 1856, p. 278, Register of Letters Received, Department of Texas, Record Group 393 (National Archives, Washington, D.C.); Greene, *Historic Resource Study*, 56–57; McDowell to Lee, Jan. 2, 31, 1857, Letters Sent, Department of Texas, 1856–58 (microfilm; National Archives); Statement of Jones, June 4, 1857 (microfilm; FODA).

12. Journal of Beale, July 16–18, 1857, H. Exec. Doc. 124, 35th Cong., 1st sess. (Serial 959), pp. 25–26; Lewis Burt Lesley (ed.), *Uncle Sam's Camels: The Journal of May Humphreys Stacey supplemented by the Report of Edward Fitzgerald Beale (1857–1858)* (1929; rpt., Glorieta: Rio Grande Press, 1970), 64.

13. Thomas L. Connelly, "The American Camel Experiment: A Reappraisal," *SHQ*, LXIX (Apr., 1966), 442–462.

14. Crimmins (ed.), "Colonel J. K. F. Mansfield's Report . . . 1856," 352–356.

15. Robert Wooster, *Soldiers, Sutlers, and Settlers: Daily Life on the Texas Military Frontier*, Clayton Wheat Williams Texas Life Series, No. 2 (College Station: Texas A&M University Press, 1987), 122–127.

16. Crimmins (ed.), "Colonel J. K. F. Mansfield's Report . . . 1856," 352–353; Edward to Father, Apr. 3, 1857, Hartz Papers.

17. Thomas T. Smith, "Fort Inge and Texas Frontier Military Operations," *SHQ*, XCII (Aug., 1992), 2–7.

18. Smith to Cooper, Oct. 9, 1854 (microfilm; FODA); Walker to Gibbs, Oct. 6, 1854, ibid.

19. Clary (ed.), "'I Am Already Quite a Texan,'" 55.

20. "Proceedings of a Board of Officers . . . ," Aug. 5, 1857 (microfilm; FODA).

21. Report of Hartz, July 30, 1857, Hartz Papers; General Orders No. 14, Nov. 13, 1857, Secretary of War, Annual Report, S. Exec. Doc. 11, 35th Cong., 1st sess. (Serial 920), 56–57.

22. Marvin E. Kroeker, *Great Plains Command: William B. Hazen in the Frontier West* (Norman: University of Oklahoma Press, 1976), vii–viii, 3, 26–30.

23. Mansfield to Thomas, Oct. 31, 1860 (microfilm; FODA); Dagmar Mariager, "Camp and Travel in Texas, I," *The Overland Monthly*, XVII (2nd ser., Feb., 1891), 188.

24. Peters to Sister, Mar. 13, 1861, DeWitt C. Peters Papers (Bancroft Library, University of California, Berkeley).

25. William H. Bell, "Ante Bellum: The Old Army in Texas in '61," *Magazine of History*, III (Feb., 1906), 81–82; Thomas Wilhelm, *History of the Eighth U. S. Infantry from its Organization, in 1838* (2nd ed.; [n.p.]: Headquarters, Eighth Infantry, 1873), II, 86–90.

26. Baylor to Adams, July 12, 1861, William C. Adams Papers (FODA); Draper to Lane, Aug. 8, 1861, John H. Draper File, ibid.

27. E. E. Townsend, "The Mays Massacre," *West Texas Historical and Scientific Society Publications*, No. 5 (1933), 29–43; San Antonio *Herald*, Sept. 7, 1861; Draper to Lane, Oct. 4, 1861, Draper File.

28. Martin Hardwick Hall, *Sibley's New Mexico Campaign* (Austin: University of Texas Press, 1960); *War of the Rebellion: A Compilation of the Official Records of the Union and Confederate Armies* (series 1), L, pt. I, 942.

29. *War of the Rebellion* (series 1), IX, 577–579; Clayton Williams, *Texas' Last Frontier: Fort Stockton and the Trans-Pecos, 1861–1895*, ed. Ernest Wallace (College Station: Texas A&M University Press, 1982), 49–57.

30. Jack D. Foner, *Blacks and the Military in American History: A New Perspective* (New York: Prager Press, 1974), 52–53.

31. Merritt to Moore, July 1, 1867 (microfilm; FODA); Report of Sherman, Nov. 20, 1870, *Secretary of War, Annual Report*, H. Exec. Doc. 1, pt. 2, 41st Cong., 3rd sess. (Serial 1446), 31.

32. Greene, *Historic Resource Study*, 115–116, 132–134; Post Medical Returns, p. 9 (FODA).

33. Gordon Chappell, *Search for the Well-Dressed Soldier, 1865–1890: Developments and Innovations in United States Army Uniforms on the Western Frontier*, Museum Monograph No. 5 (Arizona Historical Society, 1972).

34. Robert M. Utley, *Frontier Regulars: The United States Army and the Indian, 1866–1891* (New York: Macmillan, 1973), 70–73.

35. John C. Reid, *Reid's Tramp, or a Journal of Ten Months Travel Through Texas, New Mexico, Arizona, Sonora, and California* . . . (1858; rpt., Austin: Steck Co., 1935), 123; Mansfield to Thomas, Oct. 31, 1860 (microfilm; FODA).

36. Post Adjutant to Chaney, Nov. 27, 30, 1874, Jan. 7, 1875 (microfilm; FODA); Andrews to Belknap, Mar. 19, 1875, ibid.; Applicants for Post Trader, Registers of Post Traders, Record Group 94 (National Archives); ibid., XXXVII; Greene, *Historic Resource Study*, 216.

37. Edward M. Coffman, *The Old Army: A Portrait of the American Army in Peacetime, 1784–1898* (New York: Oxford University Press, 1986), 396–398; John V. Lauderdale Letterbooks, July 12, 1888 (Beinecke Rare Book and Manuscript

Library, Yale University; microfilm copy in FODA); E. O. Parker to J. W. Edwards, Mar. 27, 1973, Charles Mulhern, Enlisted Men File (FODA).

38. Darlis A. Miller, *Soldiers and Settlers: Military Supply in the Southwest, 1861–1885* (Albuquerque: University of New Mexico Press, 1989), 70–71; *Presidio County News,* May 31, 1884; Thompson, *History of Marfa and Presidio County,* I, 137, 143, 183, 198–199, 202, 205, 252, 270, 278.

39. Manuscript Returns, Ninth Census (1870) and Tenth Census (1880), Presidio County, Texas (microfilm; Corpus Christi Public Library); unsigned report, Dec. 10, 1886, Fort Davis Records, Record Group 393 (National Archives).

40. R. D. Holt, "Texas Had Hot County Elections," *West Texas Historical Association Year Book,* XXIV (1948), 11; *Army and Navy Journal,* June 5, 1885; Thompson, *History of Marfa and Presidio County,* I, 259; Lauderdale Letterbooks, Nov. 1, 1888.

41. Andrews to Assistant Adjutant General, Jan. 4, 1875 (microfilm; FODA); Crimmins (ed.), "Colonel J. K. F. Mansfield's Report . . . 1856," 354; Mansfield to Thomas, Oct. 31, 1860 (microfilm; FODA).

42. Douglas C. McChristian, *Garrison Tangles in the Friendless Tenth: The Journal of First Lieutenant John Bigelow, Jr., Fort Davis, Texas* (Bryan: J. M. Carroll and Co., 1985), 30–35; Douglas C. McChristian, *An Army of Marksmen: The Development of U.S. Army Marksmanship in the Nineteenth Century* (Fort Collins: Old Army Press, 1981).

43. James O. Breeden, "Health of Early Texas," *SHQ,* LXXX (Apr., 1977), 362–364; Statement of Jones, June 4, 1857 (microfilm; FODA); Greene, *Historic Resource Study,* 229.

44. Lauderdale Letterbooks, Aug. 22, Sept. 6, 1889.

45. Coffman, *The Old Army,* 348–349; Wooster, *Soldiers, Sutlers, and Settlers,* 107.

46. Bill dated May 1, 1885 (microfilm; FODA); Wooster, *Soldiers, Sutlers, and Settlers,* 64–68.

47. Morrison to Post Adjutant, Jan. 31, 1884 (microfilm; FODA).

48. Manuscript Returns, Ninth Census (1870) and Tenth Census (1880), Presidio County, Texas (microfilm; Corpus Christi Public Library); Sandra L. Myres, "Romance and Reality on the American Frontier: Views of Army Wives," *Western Historical Quarterly,* XIII (Oct., 1982), 409–427; Lydia Spencer Lane, *I Married a Soldier; or, Old Days in the Old Army* (1894; rpt., Albuquerque: Horn and Wallace, 1964), 22.

49. Sis to Mother, July 16, 1890, Thompson Files (FODA); Mrs. James K. Thompson to Gram and Mother, [Oct.] Nov. 3, 1890, ibid.

50. Mullins to Adjutant General, Nov. 1, 1875, Mar. 21, 1877, Appointments, Commission, and Personal Branch, Record Group 94 (National Archives); Foner, *Blacks and the Military,* 58–59.

51. Lauderdale Letterbooks, Feb. 22, July 10, 1889; Robert F. Bluthardt, "Baseball on the Military Frontier," *Fort Concho Report,* XIX (Spring, 1987), 20–21.

52. *Army and Navy Journal,* Oct. 14, 1882.

53. Grace Paulding Memoirs, p. 10 (Texas Tech University Library, Lubbock); Erwin Thompson, "The Officers, Fort Davis, Texas," Officers File (FODA); McChristian, *Garrison Tangles in the Friendless Tenth*, 26; William H. and Shirley A. Leckie, *Unlikely Warriors: General Benjamin H. Grierson and His Family* (Norman: University of Oklahoma Press, 1984), 280; Mills to Grierson, Oct. 1, 1882, Benjamin Grierson Papers (Illinois State Historical Library, Springfield).

54. Edward to Father, June 24, 1856, Hartz Papers; Manuscript Returns, United States Eighth Census (1860), Presidio County, Texas (microfilm; Corpus Christi Public Library); Foner, *Blacks and the Military*, 53–55, 60.

55. Raymond Philip Ifera, "Crime and Punishment at Fort Davis, 1867–1891" (M.A. thesis, Sul Ross State College, 1974); Coffman, *The Old Army*, 371 n. 95; Report of Proctor, Nov. 23, 1889, *Secretary of War, Annual Report*, H. Exec. Doc. 1, pt. 2, 51st Cong., 1st sess. (Serial 2715), 9.

56. Theodore D. Harris (ed.), *Negro Frontiersman: The Western Memoirs of Henry O. Flipper* (El Paso: Texas Western College Press, 1963); Barry C. Johnson, *Flipper's Dismissal* (London: privately printed, 1980); Bruce J. Dinges, "Court-Martial of Lieutenant Henry O. Flipper," *The American West*, IX (Jan., 1972), 12–17, 59–60.

57. Geddes to Rucker, Mar. 16, 1870 (microfilm; FODA).

58. Merritt to Morse, Sept. 15, 1868, photocopies of Letters Sent (FODA); Erwin Thompson, "The Negro Soldiers on the Frontier: A Fort Davis Case Study," *Journal of the West*, VII (Apr., 1968), 219.

59. "Tabular Statement of Expeditions and Scouts Against Indians," Fort Davis Records (National Archives).

60. Andrews to Commanding Officer, Dec. 10, 11, 1876 (microfilm; FODA).

61. Bruce Dinges, "Victorio Campaign of 1880: Cooperation and Conflict on the United States-Mexico Border," *New Mexico Historical Review*, LXII (Jan., 1987), 81–94.

62. General Orders No. 1, District of the Pecos, Feb. 7, 1881, Benjamin Grierson Letters and Documents (Newberry Library, Chicago; microfilm copy, FODA).

63. Grierson to Alice, May 31, 1878, Grierson Papers; Mary L. Williams, "Empire Building: Colonel Benjamin H. Grierson at Fort Davis, 1882–1885," *West Texas Historical Association Year Book*, LXVI (1985).

64. Alice to Grierson, Oct. 2, 1883, Benjamin Grierson Papers (Texas Tech University Library). The "Viele house" referred to quarters once occupied by the Tenth Cavalry's Capt. Charles D. Viele.

65. Bruce Dinges, "Colonel Grierson Invests on the West Texas Frontier," *Fort Concho Report*, XVI (Fall, 1984), 6–11.

66. Grierson to Adjutant General, Jan. 30, Mar. 16, 1883 (microfilm; FODA); R. C. Drum, "Case of Proposed Purchase of Additional Land at Fort Davis, Texas," Nov. 6, 1883, ibid. ; Drum to Commanding General, Division of the Missouri, Nov. 19, ibid.

67. Stanley to Schofield, Nov. 26, 1884, John M. Schofield Papers (Library of Congress); Stanley to Adjutant General, Dec. 19, 1884, XXIII, 74–75, Letters Sent, Department of Texas (microcopy; National Archives); Leckie and Leckie, *Unlikely Warriors*, 306–308.

68. Report of Stanley, Sept. 4, 1886, Secretary of War, Annual Report, H. Exec. Doc. 1, pt. 2, 49th Cong., 2nd sess. (Serial 2461), 126.

69. Lauderdale Letterbooks, June 23, 1886.

70. Stanley to Adjutant General, Nov. 18, 1887, XXVI, 316, Letters Sent, Department of Texas (microcopy; National Archives).

71. Proctor to Lanham, Apr. 27, 1891, Redfield Proctor Papers (Proctor Free Library, Proctor, Vermont); Proctor to Sayres, Apr. 25, ibid.

72. Murphy to Blaine, May 15, 1891 (microfilm; FODA); Schofield to Reagan, Jan. 13, 1890, XXIX, 335, Letters Sent, Headquarters of the Army (microcopy; National Archives); Schofield to Lanham, Jan. 10, 25, Mar. 18, June 2, 1890, pp. 333–334, 356, XXX, 408–409, 458, ibid.; Schofield to Secretary of War, Mar. 3, 1890, Schofield Papers.

73. Stanley to Adjutant General, July 30, 1891, XXIX, 408–410, Letters Sent, Department of Texas (microcopy; National Archives); Martin to Commanding Officer, June 1, 1891 (microfilm; FODA).

74. Mulhern to Maxon, June 30, Aug. 31, 1891, Mason M. Maxon Papers (FODA).

75. Greene, *Historic Resource Study*, 51.